Juliet C. Dorris-Williams, MSW, LISW-S

Leaving Church, Finding Faith:

Six Steps for Finding Your Purpose in the
World After Leaving the Christian Church

Juliet Dorris-Williams, MSW, LISW-S

Sacred
Essence
Press

ISBN 978-0-578-65477-5 [paperback]

First Printing July 2020

Table of Contents

Part One

Chapter 1: Go or Stay – The Cost

First, this isn't a church-bashing book. It's an unpacking. An unlearning even. Because nobody makes the decision to leave "church" willy-nilly. Leaving church is a deep ground shaking experience for those of us who have taken that step. One only takes a life-altering step like this when remaining on seemingly terra firma is no longer an option. This is a book, a story, about leaving one thing, and finding another. We must first start by examining the why. We must walk through that process of getting to … I left the Christian Church.

Like any major life decision, weighing the cost, the pro and the con, is a worthy exercise. In this instance, if you are reading these words, you've already made the decision. You may not have acted on it; but decisions like this are about alignment and surrender.

Surrender is a familiar term for people of faith. This is the vernacular we use to describe yielding ourselves to the God of our understanding. It is about an acknowledgment that our life before was unfulfilling, unworkable, unfocused, and we had come to the end of what we then knew. Joining with others who have come to that same inner destination creates connection. It is that connection that builds commitment, creates common focus, a common language, a common world view, and a common way of interacting with the world. If you are like me, you immersed yourself into that connection. So much so that when the bottom falls out, it is the connection that holds. Such is the nature of community.

Therein lies the challenge, as well as the cost. The person who yielded themselves into this community is not the same person who is weighing the cost to stay or go. You've learned and incorporated some things. You've changed, grown, deepened your concept of self. You know more about yourself and the journey that led you to this place. Most importantly, with this immersion, much like a baptism, you have emerged from the seemingly unworkable life you were living before to new life, new love, and a new sense of purpose that is grounded in gratitude, forgiveness, the pursuit of holiness, and wholeness. Communion, if you will. This is Communion. Communion and unity; with your creator and unity with the community of others; who like you, took this journey, to this place called church, and called it home.

This book is ultimately about leaving home. It is not about leaving communion.

Getting to the decision is about weighing the cost. What is it costing you to stay?

To examine the cost, you must remember what you felt, what you gained. It is often those thoughts that keep us stuck.

To discover what it is costing you to stay, we must examine what you gained by affiliating with church globally, and this particular church community in the up close and personal. It is my belief that we all crave love and belonging. I believe, along with numerous sociological and psychological research studies, we are hardwired for community. It is something that we need, something that we crave. We are simply not built for isolation. With respect to church, the institution of Christian church, we are "welcomed in ... just as we are". I believe this is something that all humans crave, simply the human condition, to be welcomed, just as we are. Sadly, it seems that once we are welcomed in, there is another process afoot. Another thing that is very much human nature is the socialization process of forming and norming of our actions, our thoughts, and our behaviors. Just as we were welcomed "just as we were", there is another process of assimilation happening. This is neither good nor bad. For some of us, this unconscious process of joining, forming and norming can bury those parts of ourselves that make us uniquely us. For others of us, it's a perfect fit. This book is not for them.

Ask yourself, what is/was it costing you to stay? If you are like me, it was costing you your sense of focus and grounding. It was costing you, YOU. You no longer "fit" into this community, this somewhat cloistered from the world institution called the church. Your love for God, Jesus and the Holy Spirit is intact. Your love for who you consider God's people is intact. Stronger even because, for you, what you now understand as "God's People" is simply without boundaries. This simple fact is the cost. What the church is supposed to be – feels small and constricting. What was a natural flow when you first joined the "community of believers" now feels stagnant, unmoving, unyielding to the flow of what for you, has been the flow of the Holy Spirit. What happens to a stagnant, unmoving body of water? It becomes a breeding ground for bacteria, mold, mosquitos etc. Things that can make you sick if consumed. What happens over time to things that make you spiritually sick? The church, which is also referenced as "the body of Christ," for you, dear reader, has become like a stagnant body of water – no movement. Or, perhaps the movement is not in a flow that feeds you. You are no longer in alignment with that flow. So – do you keep going with that flow, knowing that you are floating on the surface like a discarded leaf? What are the implications of floating along in a flow that no longer feeds or nurtures you?

The decision to go is made, or you wouldn't have picked up this book. I'm glad you did. What follows in the next chapters is my process and tumult behind leaving the Christian Church. Much of this is about my experience: what led me to this decision; how I came to peace with the decision; how I have zero regrets about the decision. By sharing my experience, I wish to help you accomplish the same.

Chapter 2: Why I Left

Thoughts about what it was costing me to stay, what would I gain to continue to serve in my usual fashion, remaining in quiet community, cocooned in an environment that was both safe but also restricting in many ways, is what weighed on me on my journey out of the Christian Church. First, I should distinguish between Christian Church as Institution, and Christian Church as "the body of Christ." I walked away from the institution. My faith, informed by my relationship with the God of my understanding, with Jesus Christ as the model, with the Holy Spirit as my teacher, remains. Some would say that my faith, as thus described, means that I am of the body of Christ, also referenced as the church universal. Others would call that a form of heresy. I remember the moment that I ceased being interested in arguing that point. Or any point having to do with how we describe God, or how we reference the work of the Holy Spirit in the world. That moment arrived before I physically left.

My leaving began on the last Sunday service of 2011. It was Christmas Day. As a long-standing churchy girl this should have been one of my high holy days. A day of being at the church I loved with a community of people I loved celebrating the birth of the *one* that was the reason for why we all were in the same space on that arguably the most important day in Christendom; when the light of God pierced the darkness of the world, and all that. High holy, high meaning, high symbolism. Yet, that day I was numb to the pageantry. I was numb to the familiar, formerly comforting words, numb to the message. Unmoved by the ritual of communion. In hindsight, I left church on that day. A high holy day.

Just over two months before, my ordination committee declined to recommend me for the next level of ordained ministry in the Christian denomination that I called my home and my heart. It was a rather stunning end to something I had been working toward for several years. The journey to ordained ministry was in response to a call, as all soul journeys are. Not my first call, but the *one* call that meant I could not turn away from this path, as challenging as it was at times. This journey included lots of mentors, some good, some not. Seminary: not what I expected, but instructive, grounding, and affirming, nonetheless. Even with the challenges I did not feel "released" to quit. Nor did it ever occur to me to do so. Just another challenge to rise to. And with the gentle nudging of the Holy Spirit, a source and force I look to and lean toward, I continued. Until I was summarily dismissed from that path by a group of people who didn't know me, nor I them.

As there were a number of people who prayed with and for me during this process, sharing the news that I would not be moving forward as ordained clergy with the church of my heart, would be the only time that I would allow space for my feelings. These people, my prayer support people, walked with me on this entire journey, and they knew me. I could not put on a brave face for them. However, I am a good social worker, as well as a trauma survivor, who has some skills in compartmentalizing my feelings. I put on my social worker hat and I dealt with all the anger, all the disappointment and all the hurt *for* me. I did a pretty good job of dealing with their emotions. Not my own. The numbness was accompanied by a sense of helplessness. My mentors were heartbroken for me, but they had no advice, no suggested steps to take. It was just over. Go with God. Go with love.

And so, I went. Out. Away. I thought at first that it was just that church, rather than *the Church*. I wandered around for several months. Different churches, different worship services and styles. From denomination to non, from small to large. From "high church" to casual. I even stayed with a newish church community for several months with other wanderer types seeking community. I geared up, or maybe geared in with this community for a time. I was seen. I was accepted. Space was made for my natural and spiritual gifts. That was a bit of a respite from my wandering in the desert longing for ritual, sameness, for like-minded community, embracing the way of Jesus and the work of the Holy spirit in changing, and empowering us to change the world. Unfortunately, it was a fragile community that could not hold together when a major change in leadership occurred.

When the end came for that small church community, I no longer wandered. I was simply done with gearing up and gearing in. One day months after, I realized that I had not visited a church nor felt a desire to do so. No more wandering. No more wondering what the church had for me, or what I could do with or for the church. No more sense of loss or purposelessness. Why? Perhaps because I realized that I was walking into my purpose every day with the job I have, working with people living with mental health, addiction and trauma challenges. My "why" for doing this work was the same as my "why" for doing the work in or on behalf of the church. I had the opportunity to serve God's people, just as they were. Every day. Everyday ministry! I was doing the pure work of Christian service, in a secular environment, as a Social Worker, where the building up of one's faith is not necessarily the point as much as it is, or could be, a byproduct of the journey. The work that I do is focused around healing, growth, and recovery. More, it is often about discovering meaning and purpose to one's life experience, one's life journey. Many of the pieces and parts of doing ministry were happening every day. Yet the focus was only indirectly pointed toward matters of the spirit, which for me, are substantial, focusing, grounding, and intentional. Ministry? Yes. Christian ministry? Not in a direct fashion. Unpacking those questions is a part of my ongoing journey.

Chapter 3:   The Lesson in the Leaving

So, you've left the church or you're contemplating your path to leave. Church is grounding. Church is purposeful. As a God-focused person, serving God in the church is a life goal. Your entire identity is built around this community. However, I do believe that is where many of us confuse our grounding for a place, rather than a journey. A parable in the book *The Dream Giver* by Bruce Wilkinson tells the story of "Ordinary" who decides to leave the "Land of Familiar" to pursue his "Big Dream." He sets off on a sometimes difficult and sometimes rewarding journey. There is conflict. There is joy. There are many obstacles. Overcoming those obstacles, even from loved ones, was difficult. Working through the challenges, made him stronger for the journey. A big lesson for Ordinary, in his pursuit of his Big Dream, was to not get too comfortable. In order to continue his journey, he sometimes had to leave behind comfort of the familiar. Like Ordinary, some of us must leave the comfort of the familiar to realize our big dream, our heartfelt desire, our Call.

It is my supposition that people make big life changing moves only when it is uncomfortable, painful or otherwise difficult to stay where they are. We make changes when remaining on the current path is no longer sustaining us or feeding us. Essentially, we make a change when NOT changing is no longer the option we are willing to live with.

For me, that journey was about peeling off layers of assimilation, unpacking life trauma, and being open to experiencing the world differently, without the comfort and the affirmation of a community that I've relied on as foundational to my life. It was as much a turning inward to better hear the guidance of the Holy Spirit, as much as it was a face forward, one foot in front of the other, turning into the wind of whatever the world presented. It was about finding new grounding while standing on a people mover machine. I know that I was headed somewhere, to do some important thing, with people I have yet to meet, with no solid goal in mind. I know that I must keep going, and the opportunities to serve will present themselves. Meanwhile, the un-layering process will be simultaneous to the journey. There will be lessons in the leaving. Lessons that will only make sense as I continue on the path.

You've left the church. The thing that focused you and gave you purpose. Finding your purpose is all about finding yourself. In order to find yourself, sometimes you must shed the layers of all those things that you geared up for and leaned in to. Finding purpose should not be confused with finding your passion. Sometimes it is simply doing the very next thing. Sometimes it is simply following your curiosity. This will lead you to people, to places and things that you will find purposeful. Because, dear friend, if you have the desire to love God and to serve God's people, the very world is your church.

Part Two

Chapter 4: The Lessons in the Wilderness

You've been working and moving toward this destination for several years. The destination (ordained ministry in the church of your heart) is within your eye view. Suddenly a brick wall appears. *Stop do not pass.* Where is my detour? Where is my off ramp? What am I supposed to do now? What is my new destination? Welcome to the wilderness.

In Chapter 2, I discussed wandering from church community to church community during the first couple of years after I left the church of my heart. In retrospect, I now know that this was a time to shed the layers of conformity that I had very willingly submitted to for the purpose of community and affiliation. A scripture comes to mind, "Do not be conformed to this world, but be transformed by the renewing of your minds, so that you may discern what is the will of God—what is good and acceptable and perfect." (Romans 12.2, New Revised Standard Version) takes on a new meaning and a new relevance when one is on the outside of the institution. I wonder now how much of me was conforming to institution rather than responding to church universal.

By church universal (my own term), I mean everybody, everywhere. For that is what I discovered, or re-discovered, when my path to ordained ministry was cut off. I discovered that my heart's intention to serve God by serving God's people was an everyday, every-encounter kind of deal. It took me a while to connect those dots as I was very much conformed to institution.

My personal journey through the wilderness wasteland of shedding layers of conformity was not a simple thing. Apparently, you can take the girl out of the church, but can't take the church out of the girl. Not without a lot of inner work that is.

The wilderness is the ongoing journey to yourself and to your call to serve. The call to Christian service comes out of one's devotion to one's faith. The wilderness is not a place you can fly over. It is a place where all your previous assumptions will be challenged. It is a place where you will see the church universal in front of you every day. It will be the place where you must choose to suit up as it will bring to you opportunities to practice your faith out loud, in real time, with real people in need of grace – unmerited favor – that you yourself understand down to your molecules. You don't even have to go looking for it. It will come to you. Dietrich Bonhoeffer, a German pastor, and anti-Nazi dissident said, "We must learn to regard people less in light of what they do or omit to do, and more in the light of what they suffer." Church institution encourages conformity as the price for grace which is antithetical to the concept of grace.

For me, the process of conformity was lifesaving. I've been a churchy girl for most of my life. Church was the one place that felt safe. Until it didn't. This last time of leaving church wasn't my first. The first time I left church was when my first marriage was ending due to abuse and trauma. My then church community was super conservative in their belief systems about gender roles and an abusive marriage did not release anyone from their "purpose" of loving their spouse into the person that God wanted them to be.

Leaving church that time also meant leaving God. I could not reconcile serving a God that would require me or my child to remain in an abusive situation. So, I left all of it behind. For a while. There was no wandering in search of a new church community. There was just done. Over and Out. The thing that I know about grace now, is that it pursues you. I left church, *and God*, and God said, "Not so fast, daughter. I have some other things I need to show you, to teach you." God didn't say that in words. But the situations and circumstances I kept finding myself in were saying that loud and clear. Nearly two years later, I walked in to the first church that would become the church of my heart. I walked into the arms of a nurturing, caring and embracing community. A community that I may never have left had it not been the need for this single mom to work *one* job that supported her and her daughter.

Sadly, and interestingly, that job was in a completely different state. Leaving the nurturing, caring, and embracing community was my second trip through the wilderness.

Just like "Ordinary" my journey through the wilderness was fraught with challenges and obstacles, not the least of which was my desire to find a new nurturing, caring and embracing community. It was also my first lesson in shedding the desire for something that would not serve me in the now. So, a community that was welcoming was good enough. I learned that many aren't. Having come from a nurturing church community, it was often disarming and uncomfortable to walk into a new church and to be either ignored, made spectacle of because you were a visitor or just to have otherwise unspecified vibes indicating, nope, not the place for you.

The wilderness allows you to expand your perspective. When you are confronted by everything but what you expect, you learn to adjust your expectations. My journey to finding connection was met by the multiple church communities I planted myself in. In retrospect, until I finally landed in the heart church, it was like being a stranger in a strange land. I joined. I learned. I volunteered my time, my talents, and my resources. Never a pew sitter. I was never content to show up to soak of the spirit. I was always an active and participating learner. I was often surprised when the leaders approached me for this role or that role. I showed up. I made myself available for service and was happy about it. I was never one to seek a leadership role, yet it always seemed to find me. Happy and grateful to serve; and when the clear knock, knock, knock on my spirit came, inviting me to do this other thing that I was not seeking, it was more like an old question. A question that I had been sidestepping, but now was finally answering. Yes. Yes. Of course. Amen.

The wilderness has levels. I went to a deeper level in the wilderness. So much so that I forgot for a time that I was still in the wilderness. There was so much to see and learn. So much to do. Such is the nature of church. It is said that 80 percent of the work is accomplished by 20 percent of the people. I was always in the 20 percent. Sometimes I was in the 10 percent. This was not burdensome. I was called. I was answering. Yes. Yes. Of course. Amen.

Answering the call though, meant learning a new language, a way to talk about God that was familiar, yet not. It meant a deeper dive into our holy book. Learning about the culture and the language of the people of the book. Learning about the history, as documented by corroborating or parallel historical resources. Seminary was both frustrating and fun. It was like taking apart a timepiece, a clock, to see the gears and how they all fit together to help humans mark time. Except it wasn't that simple. Seminary is a place to deconstruct all you think you know about your faith, and to put it back together again in a new way. You go in as one thing. You come out as another. It both affirmed my faith, and decimated my certainty about the history, the stories, the parables that had built my faith.

What I knew for sure in those moments, was that my faith was built more on the certainty that God was. The certainty that Jesus is. The inner knowing that my steps were guided by a presence that I call the Holy Spirit. I *knew* that miracles happened. I *knew* that prayers work. I *knew* that I was a loved daughter of the most high God. That is very experiential and not something that can be taught or learned. It is an experience. I had had a few. Things I can't explain. Those things, those experiences were affirmed again and again during my seminary training and through the parallel track of ordained ministry. Eventually though, there came a point where I was being asked to articulate my faith, and my call, and I failed to do so in ways that resonated with those who made the decisions as to who would be allowed to represent the heart church as ordained clergy. This is when I was reminded. Oh yeah ... still in the wilderness.

So, like "Ordinary," I continued down the road in search of "my big dream," though now, I wasn't precisely sure what that was.

Chapter 5:   Grief and Loss

Leaving church was disorienting. My life, my heart was grounded in church context. What I mean by church context is simple. There's a schedule. Beyond the usual Sunday school, Sunday worship, there is the midweek study. There are liturgical colors and seasons. There are the high holy days of Christendom, Christmas, Easter, Pentecost. I was steeped in the tradition. I loved it. It added a visual to things I really couldn't express in words. The words of scripture would suffice. Then of course there was the monthly or weekly Eucharist, known as Holy Communion or The Lord's Supper. One of most fulfilling moments in church was when I was tasked with serving or officiating. Even now, writing these words, I am filled with love about those moments. For me, it was the ultimate in service. Saying those words, while offering the bread, the body of Christ *given* for *you*, and those other words, while offering the juice (or wine) the blood of Christ *poured out* for *you*, was powerful – vertical and horizontal – connection medicine.

For months after leaving the heart church I visited other churches just for a dose of that connection medicine. Which is wonderful that, for the church communities I wandered into, I could go and participate, a stranger off the street. Granted this was much more comfortable in the mega churches where there are too many people for the leaders to know everyone. Still, I got what I needed to continue my journey. When I decided to sit awhile and check out the surroundings, I was quickly disabused of hanging around long. Churches have their own rhythms. And when you know what your rhythm is, no need to try to dance to anyone else's music.

Still, I knew that on some level I was grieving the loss of heart connection with the community I bonded with. Note, this bonding was not with the people in the one church building. Although they were lovely, the bonding was with the structure, with the organization, with the guiding, organizing, and the founding principles of the larger structure, the denomination. I had dug down deep. The deeper I went, the more in love I was. Walking away was like being kicked out of your home. It was like leaving a relationship. It was like cutting out a piece of yourself and leaving it behind.

I grieved. Or so I thought. I had (have) a wonderful job in the secular world that allowed me to serve God and serve God's people (*EVERYONE*). But it was the secular world where the practice of faith is more private, more nuanced. Yet, when faith is your home base, you are always in the faith game. You are always doing the work of faith.

While I was re-orienting to the world without church in it, other things in the world happened. Loved ones died. Catastrophes happened. Family crises happened. Life happened. You deal. Until you don't.

There were layers upon layers of life happening that pushed me into the therapist's office to work on why I wasn't sleeping. It was six months of biweekly sessions before I got to the leaving church part. I still remember my therapist staring at me and adjusting her posture in her chair when I shared that little nugget of information. To which she quietly responded, "You've not mentioned that before."

And so, down the rabbit hole we went to the bottom of my grief and the reason I wasn't sleeping. We stayed there a good while. Months even. Unpacking what all of that meant to this church girl. My therapist had/has a Christian orientation, so, once we got to that conversation, it was easy shorthand to share with her about my church experience. I did not have to orientate her to the process of ordained ministry. I did not have to overly explain the devastation I felt. Once we finally got down to it, we peeled off the layers of life that were preventing me from pulling myself out of the hole of depression that was deeper than I believed, only manifesting as an inability to sleep. I highly recommend having a therapist on speed dial. I'm only kidding a little.

For me, being able to trust the process of un-layering, with someone who was attentive, spoke my language, who could challenge the stories I was telling myself about failure, loss and grief, is invaluable. It was there that I finally was able to release myself from the burden of believing somehow that I had failed. That I had somehow failed the test. Failed God even by not being "good enough" for ordained ministry in the church of my heart. *Big heavy crap* I was walking around with. For years. It was in the company of that lovely Christian woman, my therapist, that I was able to lay that burden down.

Chapter 6: Dealing with Shame and Guilt

What the hell was that about? Yeah, 'cause that was hell. I was walking around in my own personal hell. Walking around with the story I was telling myself about not being good enough, not being smart enough to figure out the string of words these virtual strangers needed me to say to convince them that I was worthy to serve God with them, as part of the community. Clergy have a bit of a special club, you know. There are rules and processes, and tests one must pass. For me, it seemed simple. Here is this process, this path, follow the steps to get to this destination. Not so. Not in my heart church. As the process was laid out (a map), it all seemed, maybe not easy, but also not difficult. Especially if you know the why. I knew why I was there. I couldn't *not* be there. Wherever else would I be or go to serve God's people in and outside of God's house. This was the process to do so, in as full a way as possible.

Those were my thoughts. I ignored things. People are people after all. People are imperfect. Systems are built by imperfect people. I was happy to join up with my fellow and sister imperfect people. Because that is who we are at the core – imperfect people looking to a perfect and loving God to lead and guide us in loving and serving other imperfect people. It's the gospel, after all. The good news, that God loves us perfectly. Come as you are. All is well. You are loved, welcomed, and accepted. Again, my thoughts, my orientation, my belief system that carried me to this place in time, where I am sitting in front of people with the power to advance me to the next level of the ordination process. It never occurred to me that we, them and me, were operating from a different orientation all together. My orientation was about serving God's people wherever I found them, meeting them just as they are, freely extending grace. In retrospect, I suspect that their orientation was more focused on doing those same things, but "inside" the church only. It's not that we were speaking a different language, as much as we had a different focus.

My letter informing me that I would not be moving forward in the process was simple. There wasn't a lot of information that would help me discern the why of the decision. It was a gently worded letter. That had the impact of a sledgehammer on my heart. At the time I had no words to articulate the impact of that letter. Other people had words. I spent more time dealing with other people's energy surrounding me than I did my own. Now I can talk about the numbness, the deep sadness and disappointment. Now I can talk about the utter sense of rejection. Now I can talk about the despair. Now, I can talk about how it felt like I had failed God's test. Had this been *anyone* else, I would have done my level best to talk them off that crazy thinking ledge; but there was no *me* around to talk to *me* about *me*.

I walked through life for several years suppressing the emotion of that experience, while other painful life experiences layered on top. It was much easier to deal with the other stuff. Trauma survivors compartmentalize well. It's not the healthiest coping mechanism, but it can allow us to live life and not crumble, at least for a while. For some of us a long while. It works until it doesn't.

At some point I realized that I was holding my breath. Waiting to exhale. I was six, seven months into therapy when I realized this. It was years, plus those seven months before I could formulate the question out loud – why was I not able to formulate the set of words that articulated the depth of my faith and my desire to serve God and the church with my sister and fellow Christians? Why was I not enough? I had allowed the ordination committee to become *the* committee in Juliet's head; and they were taking up too much real estate.

Therapy helped me move from: Did I fail, or did I win? Therapy helped me articulate the difference between being rejected by God and being rejected by humans. I absolutely knew that I walked and remained in the presence of God through this experience. However, the emotion, the hurt, the rejection had crowded it out. I was paralyzed in my grief. Compartmentalizing the grief so that I could function through life. Still paralyzed, nonetheless. Therapy helped me name the grief, name the shame, and exhale. Therapy helped me ditch the shoulda's, oughta's and woulda's. Therapy helped me simply accept that some paths are not mine. Some outcomes are ultimately not in alignment with my highest good, my purposeful life. Therapy helped me understand that the lesson is sometimes in the journey.

Chapter 7: Resolution

It is said that when the student is ready, the teacher will appear. When I was finally in a mental and emotional space to articulate my inner devastation, I came across a quote by Maya Angelou, "You alone are enough. You have nothing to prove to anyone." This was brought home to me during one of my rabbit hole wanderings on the internet. I had become curious to know if there were books or blogs authored by people having had the same experience of being rejected for ordination. I was in new territory. On a path that I never imagined I would be walking. I was looking for community. While I didn't find community – as, at the time, there were not a lot of people writing about this – my google search began showing me what it thought was related things. "Ordination in three easy steps" is a good summation of those search results. Eventually, out of curiosity, I clicked on a few of the links. Disbelievingly, after researching one of the links for legitimacy, I followed the steps, which basically involved completing an online questionnaire, save, submit. Much to my utter surprise, within fifteen minutes or so I received a "Congratulations Rev. Juliet" email from the Universal Life Church. My first reaction was laughter. I laughed. And laughed. And laughed. It can't have been that easy, I said to myself. What, no seminary? No school loan debt? No committee? *What*?! Nothing to prove. Nothing to articulate. No need to justify my call to ministry. *What is happening*?

So, yeah, that happened. Did I feel differently? No. Did I do different things because the Universal Life Church said I was Reverend Juliet? Nope. Not yet anyway. Still waiting on someone to ask me to officiate their wedding. I can legally do so now. I'm still a little bit astonished, frankly. I worked so hard and diligently to do this the "traditional" way. To end that journey in a less than spectacular way has me still shaking my head.

It also freed me. I did not realize that I had shackled myself to one way to serve God. I had forgotten what I already knew about the life of Jesus as chronicled in the gospels. How did I not remember that Jesus was rejected by the chief priests and leaders of the temple? How did I not remember that he made himself available to the people on the margins? How did I forget that he simply ministered to the people who were around him? He cared for them. He fed them. He taught them and loved them. How did I forget the very model for service so clearly laid out in the book that we Christians call holy? So much about who I am and what I do is summed up by "go and do likewise." I was now free to go and do likewise. Not because someone said I was Rev. Juliet. Simply because of my heart desire to follow in the footsteps of the one I serve and to model his *way* – to love God with all my heart, all my soul, all my mind and all my strength – and to love my neighbor as myself. Free to be me – unshackled to any faith tradition, released to radical service and servanthood, living my life, serving the people around me, like a continuous living prayer of gratitude.

Chapter 8: Finding Ground / Finding Home / Finding Grace

It is somewhat coincidental that I would be licensed to perform certain tasks as an ordained minister from an entity with the word universal in its title. I've come to the realization that my call to Christian service is, in fact, universal. Devotion to my faith never wavered. My desire to be of service was never quenched. I have never thought of faith as a closed system, confined to creeds, doctrines, customs, or precepts of any given institution. My natural curiosity has sent me down many a rabbit hole in search of the origins of a belief system. I have stopped being surprised by the similarities.

My journey to faith freedom, as it were, is simply grounded in what I know about grace. The unmerited, unequivocal, love of God, our creator. What I know about the Christian holy books can give one a different impression. We are so often met by what I call the Old Testament messages of how we need to work for God's love. Clean up our act for God's love. Do this. Don't do that. Follow these 600 rules, and then, *maybe* then, God will consider us worthy to be loved and accepted. This is the problem with the cherry-picking process of reading the bible. We are generally not taught to read it critically. I don't know about all seminaries, but the one I attended taught me about church history, the timeline of when the Bible was written, what was left out, what might have been inserted at a later date, who was in power, and most importantly, who is speaking these words, and to whom.

* * *

As I have written in previous chapters, this time of leaving church institution was not the first time I walked away. The first time was shortly after walking away from an abusive marriage, I also walked away from God.

I was raised in a conservative fundamentalist Christian tradition. Men were the head of the household. The Christian duty of women was to graciously submit to her husband's leadership in the home. Divorce was frowned on. Homosexuality was an abomination. Women were never called to preach. Those are just a few of the highlights. None of that really mattered to me until – I divorced my abusive husband and began raising my daughter on my own. Until my social work career immersed me in the world of abused children. Until I was promoted to a job where all my friends and colleagues were in the LGBTQ community. Until several of my friends died of AIDS. Until my church decided that my single parent family wasn't a real family due to the absence of a husband/father in the home. My life path led me to reject the church and all its teachings, and God because that is allegedly where all of that came from. That's what I was taught for years.

My experience of God and grace and the wooing of the Holy Spirit began during that time of separation. It was a time of big change with the divorce and navigating life with the care and safety of a small child as my primary focus. When I talk about the wooing, I am referencing the women and men that were often in my path to offer aid, advice, direction, focus. Teachers in my daughter's school. Auto mechanics. People one encounters in work situations. Random conversations and encounters with people doing ordinary things. In the course of conversation, many of them would ask what church I attended. To which they would get the simple short answer "I don't." Then there was the inevitable invitation to visit their church some Sunday. I generally dismissed these invitations as polite conversation, until the same church name started being repeated. From different people. In random situations and circumstances. That got my attention. So much so that after nearly two years, I with my little girl in tow, walked into the doors of that church and was introduced to a loving God, and a loving community that accepted me, and us, as we were. I had been wooed. I didn't know the word for it then, but now I know it as God's grace in action. Wooing us to come close. Closer still. In those early months of being back in the fold as it were, my relationship with God deepened and grew, and I knew that I would never be the same.

That church community was grounding. A home. It was where I came to know that everything that I was about, was in service to my creator. After several years my work career took me away from my church home. Everything I came to know about God and faith I took with me. It is that grounding in faith that sustained me through the journeys ahead, that sustains me now. Everything that I later learned about prevenient grace (God's grace that comes before our awareness or before any conscious decision) was simply confirmation of what I knew to be true. Not because it had been taught to me, but because I experienced it firsthand.

As my path took me from church to church, my grounding in grace remained. Later, when that path simply had no more churches in it, grace remained. I had left the institution of church behind. God's grace was with me at every step. I left the church a second time after I was denied ordained ministry. This time, I didn't leave God. Good thing. I know for sure that God would have chased me.

Three or so years after I left church institution seemingly for good, I found myself siting in a church. Ha! I had been invited to a special installation to ministry service of a dear friend. I felt no discomfort and I wasn't numb to the movement around me. The singing was wonderful. The preached message about "God entrusting us" was inspiring. The installation process was heartwarming. The dinner later was delicious. It was a good few hours. Yet I felt no pull to return to that community. While sitting there what I did feel was inspired to type out these words into the Notes app on my phone:

"My call is not to the church. My call is to God. I give myself away in Service to serve God's will and purpose. God trusts me to serve his people (I would've typed HER people now) outside the walls. God trusts me to shepherd those placed in my path. God will order my steps and I will go. God trusts me to go. Thank you, Lord. Amen."

At the time, I called that a revelation. That was the title of my note. It was also a confirmation and more importantly an affirmation of my call to servanthood of the most high God. It was also when I stopped asking why? And just simply, quietly, renewed my yes and amen.

Chapter 9: Courage to Serve Faithfully and Freely

Brené Brown, in her book *Braving the Wilderness*, says, "Belonging is the innate human desire to be part of something larger than us. Because this yearning is so primal, we often try to acquire it by fitting in and by seeking approval, which are not only hollow substitutes for belonging, but often barriers to it. Because true belonging only happens when we present our authentic, imperfect selves to the world, our sense of belonging can never be greater that our level of self-acceptance." She goes on to say, "being ourselves means sometimes having the courage to stand alone, totally alone."

If you've reached this chapter, then that quote should be no surprise to you, as that has ultimately been where I was leading you to. This has been my journey. There were places during my journey that I believed were, in fact, my destination. Yet, circumstances, sometimes painful circumstances, propelled me to movement to the next destination. I had a reasonable expectation, from a career perspective, that moving on from one job to another was normal. I had absolutely no expectation that my journey through the institution of church would be likewise.

Church represented connection. Church represented community. Church, for me, represented safety. Safety in sameness. Church represented a shared language, a shared experience; and it was all those things. For a time. Until it wasn't. When I left church institution this second and last time, I left, not in search of any of those things that the institution meant to me. I left in search of what it means to be a person of deep faith outside of the institution that helped to nurture it. For a time, as I wandered from church to church, I was hungry for ritual. I had several opportunities to observe ritual from a variety of vantage points; and yes, the hunger was fed. For a time, I went in search of the shared experience of receiving the Eucharist. Again, from a variety of vantage points. That was not as fulfilling as I had become accustomed to the form and substance of a certain way of performing that ritual. It was educational. There were times that I was hungry for worship in song, and worship in word (preaching). Mixed experience from the various vantage points. Invariably something would occur, or something would be said that helped me know that I was no longer that person that could fit comfortably in a faith that was not expansive.

By expansive I mean, *big* faith, *radical* openness, *revolutionary* and *transformational* service and servanthood. I found that for a time, in the little church that could not hold together because of leadership change. The lesson there, is that sometimes you can get all the things you need or want, but it does not mean that you get to, or need to, keep them forever. For the brief season that I had all of that in church institution community, it was enough to, one, end my wanderings, and two, be finally done in seeking that which I already possessed. It was enough for me to know that I did not need institution to activate my call to ministry, my call to servanthood.

I was / am surrounded by people every day who need to know what grace looks like and what it feels like when it is freely offered simply because they are standing in front of me. I can freely offer it because I am freely showered and embraced with it. Grace – unmerited favor. In my chosen career of Social Work, we call that "positive unconditional regard."

What would the world look and feel like if everyone approached everyone else with "positive *unconditional* regard"; If everyone affirmed everyone else. If everyone extended love and kindness to everyone else – human to human – for no other reason except, I see you, you are worthy of being seen, you are enough. Right now. Sounds a bit like what I imagine heaven to be.

Therapy over the years helped me to excavate some abandonment issues that fed into my deep need for community. While I absolutely believe we are hardwired for community and connection, there are times and circumstances when one must stand alone. For me, my willingness to mold and shape myself to fit church structure may have been my ultimate undoing. I was being called to God's work in a more expansive way. Yet, my very human need for community and connection limited my vision and some would say my life mission. That mission, that purpose had not yet been revealed to me. Somewhat like Abraham's call story. God told Abraham to pack up and go. Go to a land I will show you. I wish I could say that I was like Abraham and I willingly packed up and started walking in the direction not knowing my destination. I would like to believe that Abraham was a regular human dude who dug in his heals for a while; but that is not how the story is written. I was dug in. Happy to be dug in. I did not want to leave the land of "familiar." Yet, had I not, my calling, to serve faithfully and freely, may not have been fully realized. Had I not, I would not have been led to home in on a life mission. Had I not, I would not have been doing the work that I do, in the way that I do. A work colleague, with whom I shared a greatly abbreviated story of why I left church, said, with tears in his eyes, "but you get to touch over 100 people's lives *every day*." He further said,

"I don't know any church that does that." Affirmation. Confirmation. Amen. Amen.

Part Three

Chapter 10: The Universal Community

There is such a thing as the Universal church. This isn't about that. There are creeds that speak to the church universal. This isn't about that either. Not exactly. When I reference the universal community, I mean humanity. All of humanity. One of the most important, most foundational biblical references is "For God so loved the world, that he gave his one and only Son, that whoever believes in him shall not perish, but have eternal life." (John 3:16, New International Version). In my wanderings across church institutions I found no disagreement about this. No argument. No debate about this being a basic tenant for Christian believers everywhere. The argument and debate appear to surround this – what does "belief" look like?

What does belief look like? Well, considering the number of churches, denominations, and religious institutions worldwide, there is a fair argument to say that we, the collective we, do not agree on what belief looks like. When we do not agree, we divide into factions. Our communities divide and split into even smaller factions. Malvina Reynolds wrote a song called "Little Boxes" in 1962. It is described as political satire about conformist middle class attitudes with respect to middle class suburbia. People in the same neighborhoods, go to the same schools, go into the same line of work – and "They all look just the same" is the refrain. Our human need for community and connection can lock us into a certain way of thinking, especially when we join with like-minded others. It doesn't have to, but in our reality, in our humanness, it often does.

My focus, even while actively engaged in church institution was "For God so loved the world...." Perhaps it was my vocation as a social worker that broadened my view. I was afforded the opportunity of exposure to different communities, different viewpoints, different ways of engaging with the world and the worlds systems. For whatever reasons, when I engaged with people, I considered them sister and fellow travelers in the world. The world that God so loved. Whatever set of circumstances or whatever mystical alchemy that occurred that had us sitting or standing across from one another, I was looking at a person that God loved, and I wanted to see that person with God's eyes.

It is easy to point to a community or a belief system and call it evil. In *Braving the Wilderness*, Brené Brown says "People are hard to hate close-up. Move in. Speak truth to bullshit. Be civil. Hold hands. With strangers. Strong back. Soft front. Wild heart." There is no better way to activate "For God so loved the world." We don't always have to believe the same or act the same or do the same things, but we would be in so much better shape as a global community if we "moved in" and did what Steven Covey suggested, "Seek first to understand, then to be understood."

The universal community then is the world that God so loves. I found that I do not want to be limited in how to engage with the universal community in acts of faith. Just as Jesus stretched out his arms on that tree and chose to remain there until his work was finished, that expression of love with no boundaries is the faith that I want to live. The world is my community. And God so loves the world. The only thing I have to offer is myself. My gifts and my talents are all the tools I have. My journey in church institution was limiting. I know that now.

When I stopped wandering from church to church, I was deeply troubled about my life purpose. However, it was in the wandering that I found it. Once I ceased to wander, I was able to shed beliefs, values, and opinions that were no longer in alignment with where I was in my spiritual journey. I developed a mission statement for myself:

"To amplify, illuminate and embrace the sacred journey toward truth and wholeness in myself and others."

I have this pinned to the bulletin board just above my home computer. Right in the middle. In big bold print. It is more than a focal point. It is a destination point for everything that I do in the world, not a physical place. A mystical place that keeps me in harmony with God so loved the world. All our journeys are sacred. The truth is what is true for each of us. There is more compatibility about that from person to person than how it appears. Especially when you move in a little closer. Wholeness. Harmony. In myself first. Then with others. I often say that you can't take anybody someplace you've never been. My mission statement reminds me of where I've been, where I'm going, and what is my ongoing, never-ending journey.

Every journey is better with peers, friends, and community. Community looks and is different on this side of leaving church. It is my hope that you have learned from me and my journey through this wilderness, and more, that it doesn't feel as lonely. Will you arrive at the exact same place I did? Probably not, but you will arrive to *your* destination. Your purposeful destination that embodies all you desire to do in service to your Creator.

Chapter 11: Being a Force of Good in the World

I know that there are many who believe that leaving church is the same as turning away from the faith. Some turn away from faith because they are buried under man-made doctrine and dogma. However, dear reader, have freed yourself and opened the door to the universality of faith, the radical and revolutionary way of service. You took a brave step picking up and reading this book. Are you braver still to walk through the door and to let go of the doorknob? The doorknob represents safety, and familiarity. Letting go is life-altering. But not life-destroying. If anything, it is life-giving.

Maya Angelou wrote, "A Woman in harmony with her spirit is like a river flowing. She goes where she will without pretense and arrives at her destination prepared to be herself and only herself."

Just like the little drummer boy who wanted to play his drum for the little Christ child, because that was all he had to give, you've been given the gift of yourself. It is all you have to give.

The purpose and practice of faith is not a closed system. My wish for you is that you will live your faith out loud – unfettered by the do's and don'ts of faith expression. My wish for you is that you will free your faith from the little boxes, and use your voice, your gifts and talents to create your platform that will be a force of good in the world. You left the church. You didn't leave God. More importantly, God didn't leave *you*. Learn – or perhaps relearn – how to rely on that "still small voice" that has always been there but is no longer drowned out by a structure that no longer serves you. Moreover – a structure that no longer allows YOU to serve.

We've walked through what it is costing you to stay in Chapter 1. Hopefully, you were able to examine and acknowledge that your sense of grounding and focus is no longer present in this environment. You no longer fit in this world called the church.

* * *

I've shared the story of why I stayed and why I left. My feelings of being ungrounded, unmoored, even resulted in my loss of purpose. In many ways it was like losing home.

We've spent some time in the wilderness. We now know this is a time and a tool for shedding the mask, relinquishing the layers of conformity that we donned for the sake of belonging and for the sense of community. It is where we learned that the wilderness does not mean that you are lost. On the contrary, the wilderness is where you will find yourself. The wilderness is where you will find affirmation and confirmation of your faith. It is the path to purpose.

We have spent some time talking about the two companions on the Wilderness road, grief and loss. It is necessary to walk with these companions, to flow with these feelings. as they are instructive for your never-ending journey of bringing your authentic self to your faith practice. It is here where you may stumble upon the realization that just because you can do a thing, does not mean you should do a thing. It's all about alignment and letting go of those things that no longer serve you.

Shame and Guilt are never helpful. You know what you know, and you make decisions based on the information accessible to you at the time. We get in our own way by carrying around internal blame and shame that is often more related to the stories we are telling ourselves rather than the reality of the actual thing. For people of faith, accepting grace for ourselves is often more difficult than extending it to others.

We talked more about that in Chapter 9 where we discovered new grounding, a new sense of home, and finally just the peace and calmness of accepting and living in grace. We learned that leaving church does not mean leaving faith behind. It means opening to purposeful, intentional, faithful and universal servanthood.

In Chapter 9 we also talked about resolve. A resolve to live into your faithful devotion to God that is with you wherever you go. The practice of faith is not a closed system, confined to creeds, doctrines, and precepts of institution. While many of those things may have guided your practice of faith within church institution, they will not, and should not box you in from a more universal practice of your faith. It may require, and I recommend, that you unpack the history of your belief systems. Where did they come from? Who was allowed input into the development? What was the political climate of the environment where it was developed? Who is speaking? To whom are they speaking? It may take a little work and a little time. I promise you, the journey of understanding what you believe and why you believe it, is worth it. Though it may shake your foundation, you will discover firm footing having gone on this journey.

Paradoxically, the courage and freedom to practice your faith by embracing all that has served you in the past, while shedding those things that did not, is not something that you arrive at easily or magically. Moving forward out of the land of the familiar, to an unknown destination, is scary. To get to the courage for the journey, you must start walking first. This is where you will lean on and into the faith you already have. It will only grow bigger, and stronger, as you continue your journey.

You may not see the world as the universal community as I do. It just means that we are not likely to walk along as companions on this road to service. However, if the concept of God so loved the world resonates with you, know that you and I are in virtual community. You are not alone.

Finally, my friend on the way, there are no mistakes, only lessons. Everything that has brought you to this moment in time is relevant and useful to your Being a Force of Good in the World. Remember that you left behind an organizing structure. You didn't leave God. Nor did God leave you. The world needs your gifts. Go forth and share them.

~JDW
December 14, 2019

Acknowledgments

To Timothy, my always and forever number one cheerleader. The one who is always nudging me forward, always shoring me up when life gets heavy, and always making me laugh when I'm being much too serious. Yes, it was in the criteria. Who knew you would be so excellent at it? I am here, at book #2, only because you pestered me. Thank you. Love you. Always.

To Tiffany Ariel, my babygirl, my other cheerleader, encourager, tech teacher, and reality checker. How in the world did we get here?? I am so proud of the woman you are, and the friends we have become. You are so unapologetically you. I am in awe of your many gifts and talents, which now includes line editing. You should now add that to your resumé. Thank you for your unwavering support. Thank you for not letting me hide or retreat. Love you. Always.

To the folks at "The Incubated Author". Life happened and I did not get to meet most of you in person. This book would not have been written had you not showed up in my path with "the authors way". I am grateful.

To my sister on the way, and former pastor, Bishop E. Anne Henning Byfield, who gently welcomed me, not just into a church community nearly 26 years ago, but unknowingly partnered in God's wooing process, by inviting me to start your "bootcamp" teaching series. It was during that immersion, that for the very first time I met and finally understood God as a perfect, fully loving and affirming parent, upon whom I could depend for my life, for my very breath. That singular, months long, experience grounded me. It carried me through the long wilderness that came after. It carries me still. Thank you. Much love.

About the Author

Juliet C. Dorris-Williams is a wife, a mother, a master's trained, licensed, social worker administrator, providing executive leadership of a peer recovery organization. Throughout her adult life, she has learned to successfully navigate the challenges that come with being a survivor of trauma and its accompanying twin, depression. Juliet credits the transformative power of her Christian faith, therapy and peer support as instrumental for her healing. This is Juliet's second published work. Find her blogs and her first book, *Notes to My 25 Year Old Self* at her website, www.julietdorriswilliams.com

Juliet was born and raised in Indianapolis, Indiana, and now lives in Reynoldsburg, Ohio with her husband, number one cheerleader and soul mate, Timothy, Sr. Their growing blended family includes four adult children, spouses, partners, grandchildren, and great grands.

Juliet is a lifelong learner with an insatiable curiosity and a seriously expensive addiction to books.

Sacred
Essence
Press

Leaving Church, Finding Faith:
Six Steps for Finding Your Purpose in the World After Leaving the
Christian Church

Juliet C. Dorris-Williams, MSW, LISW-S